W9-AOL-806

WITHDRAWN

Children's Catalog

ROCKFORD PUBLIC LIBRARY

Rockford, Illinois

www.rockfordpubliclibrary.org

815-965-9511

ROOTS

BLACKBIRCH PRESS

An imprint of Thomson Gale, a part of The Thomson Corporation

THOMSON

GALE

Detroit • New York • San Francisco • San Diego • New Haven, Conn. • Waterville, Maine • London • Munich

THOMSON
GALE
™

Consultant: Kimi Hosoume
Associate Director of GEMS (Great
   Explorations in Math and Science),
Director of PEACHES (Primary
   Explorations for Adults, Children,
   and Educators in Science),
Lawrence Hall of Science,
University of California,
Berkeley, California

For The Brown Reference Group plc
Editors: John Farndon and Angela Koo
Design Manager: Lynne Ross
Picture Researcher: Clare Newman
Managing Editor: Bridget Giles
Children's Publisher: Anne O'Daly
Production Director: Alastair Gourlay
Editorial Director: Lindsey Lowe

PHOTOGRAPHIC CREDITS
Ardea: Steve Hopkin 17; **The Brown Reference Group plc:** 19; **Corbis:** Ron Boardman /
FLPA 7, Michele Garrett 11, Robert Holmes 1, 4, Bob Krist 21, Thom Lang 8, Luca I.
Tettoni 22; **FLPA:** Jurgen & Christine Sohns 10; **Oxford Scientific Films:** Bob Bennett
12; **Photos.com:** 3b, 9, 14, 18.

Front cover: Photos.com

LIBRARY OF CONGRESS CATALOGING-IN-PUBLICATION DATA

Farndon, John.
   Roots / by John Farndon.
      p. cm. — (World of plants)
   Includes bibliographical references and index.
   ISBN 1-4103-0421-3 (lib. : alk. paper)
   1. Roots (Botany)—Juvenile literature. I. Title

   QK644.F37 2005
   575.5'4—dc22

                                                    2005047045

Printed and bound in Thailand
10 9 8 7 6 5 4 3 2 1

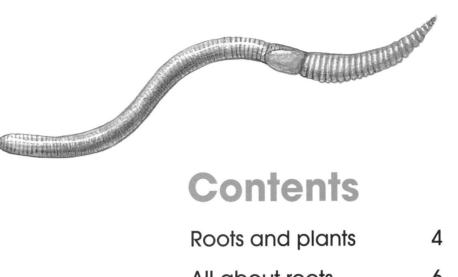

Contents

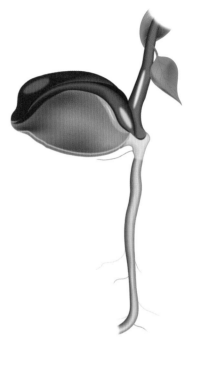

Roots and plants

Roots are the one part of a plant you hardly ever see, because they are nearly always under the ground.

▼ Cypress trees

Cypress trees live in wet places. Huge roots support the trees in soft, wet ground.

Roots are the parts of a plant that grow downward. Most plants grow their roots in soil. Water plants grow their roots down through the water. They may poke down into the mud at the bottom. A few plants have roots that hang in the air.

Roots help anchor the plant in the ground. They keep the plant from blowing away or falling over. This helps keep the leaves facing the sky.

Supply route

Roots are also a plant's supply pipes. They take up water and vital substances the plant needs from the soil.

It's Amazing!

Some roots are very tiny. Duckweed is a plant that floats on water. Its roots are thinner than the thinnest hair. Other plants have huge roots. The wild fig has the longest roots in the world. These trees live in dry places. Their roots go 380 feet (120 meters) into the ground and reach water deep down.

flower

leaf

seed pod

soil

stem

roots

◄ Plant parts

The parts of a plant above the ground are often green. Roots are generally brown or white.

5

All about roots

Roots grow from a single root and branch out below ground—just like plant stems above the ground.

When a plant starts to grow from a seed, it sends down a single root into the ground. This root is called the primary root. The primary root is the thickest root throughout the plant's life. The primary root quickly grows branches called secondary roots. Eventually the secondary roots have branches of their own.

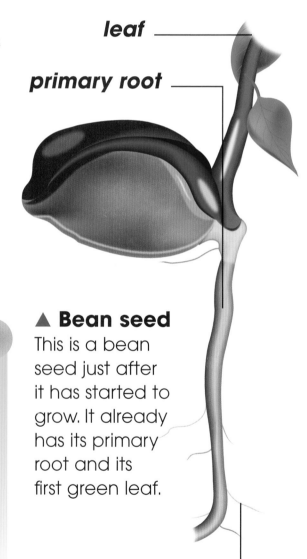

leaf

primary root

▲ Bean seed
This is a bean seed just after it has started to grow. It already has its primary root and its first green leaf.

secondary root

✦ It's Amazing! ✦

A single rye grass plant might have 7,000 miles (11,000 kilometers) of roots and root hairs. That is long enough to stretch across the United States and back again. The roots grow more than 3 miles (5 km) per day.

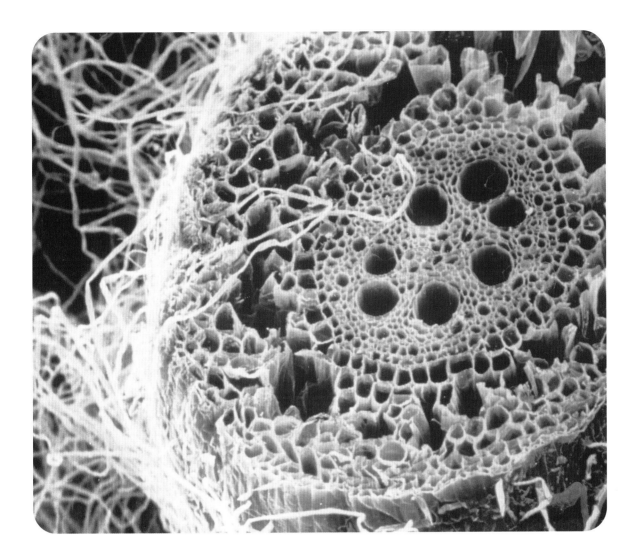

A root is made up of tiny units called cells, which are far too small to see. The root grows by adding more cells to its tip. As the root pushes through the soil, a tough cap on the tip protects these cells.

▲ Root threads

This is a slice through a root under a powerful microscope. The dark holes are pipes that carry water and food to the plant. The white fluff are tiny threads that soak up water or food from the soil.

Kinds of roots

▲ Grass roots

Grass has fibrous roots. The roots do not grow deep but form a tangled mat called turf. Turf is bound so tightly that gardeners cut squares of it from the ground—grass stems, roots, and all. People lay squares elsewhere to make a new lawn.

Roots can be many different shapes and sizes. Each type of plant has its own kind of root. Some plants have lots of small threadlike roots that spread out in all directions. These roots are called fibrous roots.

Other plants have one root much bigger than all the

others. This root is called a tap root, because it grows straight down to "tap," or pull in, water from deep in the ground.

Many trees have tap roots. When a tree starts life from a seed, the tap root is the first root to grow. Then a few days later, side roots start to grow. On trees like oaks the tap root survives for years. With most trees, though, the side roots soon take over altogether. The tap root withers and dies.

It's Amazing!

Some desert plants have deep tap roots that reach water far below ground. People in the Kalahari desert in Africa dig deep wells to get water. Once they found the tap root of a thorn tree 220 feet (70 meters) down.

leaves

tap root

stems

9

▲ Carrots
Some vegetables, like carrots, are just one big thick tap root. They grow in the ground, with just the leaves and stems poking up above the soil. The carrot plant uses its tap root to store the sugary food made by its leaves.

Special roots

Some roots have special tasks, such as helping the plant stay upright or cling to things. Corn plants, for example, sometimes have roots that start above the ground. They grow out from the stalk. They are called prop roots because they prop or hold up the plant. Prop roots keep a plant from falling over if the ground is soft or the wind is strong. Some palm trees have prop roots.

Climbing roots

Some plants, like ivy, climb everywhere. Plants that climb are called creepers. They have tiny grasping roots all along their stems. These extra roots allow them to cling to things like trees and walls.

Roots in the air

Some plants do not even grow their roots in the ground. Some types of orchids and other plants live high up on tree branches. They send out roots called aerial roots, which cling to the branch. The roots soak up water and nutrients from the air.

◄ Dangling roots

The spiky clusters are not leaves but plants growing on tree branches. These plants are called epiphytes. Epiphytes have roots that hang in the air, called aerial roots. Many orchids are epiphytes.

Try This!

Plant hyacinth bulbs in a glass pot. Bury them in soil with the point upward. Then store the pot in a warm, dark place. Keep the soil moist with water but not too wet. When the leaves are tall, bring the pot into daylight. You will see many roots in the soil like those in the picture. These roots are called adventitious roots. They grow directly from the stem. A bulb is a kind of stem.

11

Roots and animals

Many animals have a special relationship with plant roots. Some use roots as homes. Some animals eat roots.

▲ **Fox hole**
These fox pups have a safe home among the roots of a tree.

Some large animals like foxes and rabbits live in underground homes called burrows. The animals dig their burrows underneath trees. Tree roots prop up the soil as the creatures dig.

It's Amazing!

Voles love eating roots. If a gardener sees chewed roots on some trees, the chances are a vole has been at work. Two small grooves might be left by their large front teeth. Sometimes voles eat their way through the roots of a whole orchard, which makes the trees wobbly.

root vole

The roots keep the soil from caving in. If the soil caved in suddenly it would bury the animals. The roots act just like the roof timbers in houses.

Root eaters

Many small animals like roots because they make tasty and healthy food. Porcupines eat roots in summer, for example. So do gophers, squirrels, and many other similar creatures. All these animals have sharp claws for digging roots out from the soil. They also have very sharp teeth for gnawing their way through roots. Most roots are too tough for people to eat.

13

Insects and roots

▲ **Adult scarab beetle**
Young scarab beetles are wormlike grubs. They live in the soil for many years. The grubs eat roots and can damage plants.

Crawling around the roots of many plants are countless insects and other creepy crawlies. Some live in roots. Others lay their eggs on roots. Both springtails and mites feed on roots. (Unlike springtails, mites are not insects but relatives of spiders.) Insects like beetles live in the soil when young. They look like tiny worms and are called grubs, or larvae. They feed on roots until they are big enough to climb out of the soil. Only then do they change into adult insects and stop eating roots.

Real pests

Many farmers and gardeners think insects that live in the soil and feed on roots are pests. That is because the bugs can kill plants by damaging their roots.

There are three kinds of root-eating insects farmers really dislike—mole crickets, white grubs, and billbugs. Mole crickets have spadelike front legs, like moles, for digging through soil. White grubs are the grubs of scarab beetles. Billbugs are weevil larvae.

It's Amazing!

Every now and then, what look like piles of soil in the backyard start to move. They are not really soil— they are swarms of tiny insects called springtails. Springtails live in the soil and feed on roots. They get their name because their strong tails help them leap 20 times their own length. That is just like a person leaping right over a tall church tower!

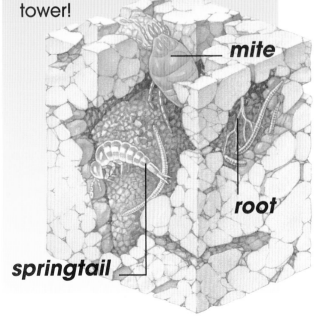

mite

root

springtail

Worms and bugs

Roots and the soil they grow in are full of tiny wriggling creatures like earthworms as well as microorganisms, which are very, very tiny life-forms too small to see. Both can often be good for the plants.

Earthworms help churn up the soil and make it easier for roots to grow. Worms keep soil from getting clogged, too, so air and water can get to roots.

Helpful microorganisms

Bacteria are microorganisms; many live in soil or roots. Some bacteria can make people ill. But many plants have bacteria called rhizobia ("ri-ZO-bee-uh") living inside their roots. The plant and the rhizobia help each other. The plant gives the rhizobia food. The rhizobia give the plant vital chemicals, such as nitrogen, that it needs to live.

★ It's Amazing! ★

As they tunnel through soil, earthworms leave a trail behind them called a casting. Castings are very rich in nutrients for plants. Sometimes, roots follow these trails of nutritious castings as they grow, even if it means growing upward!

earthworm

▶ Trillions of worms

Slithering over many roots are very, very tiny worms called nematodes. They are the most numerous creatures on Earth. There are more than 250 million in every pound of soil! This picture shows a soil nematode magnified many, many thousands of times.

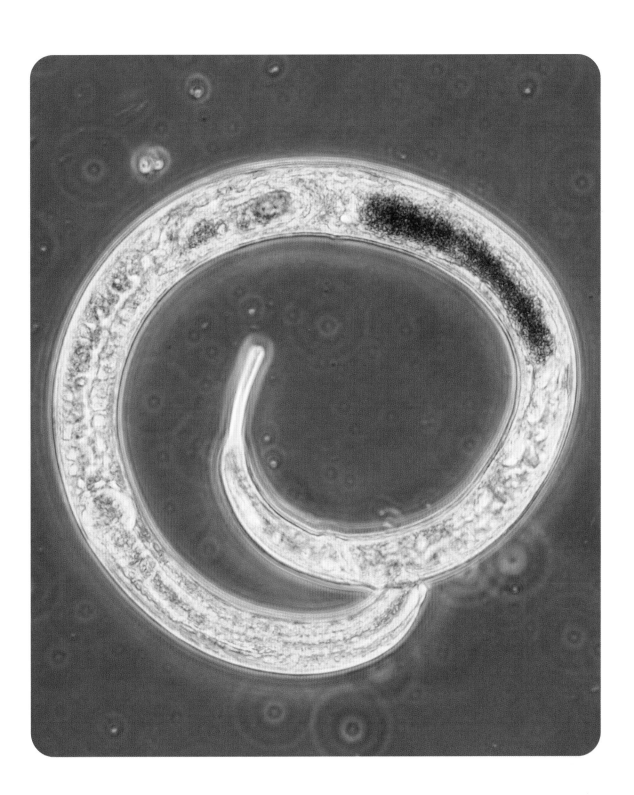

Roots and people

Roots can both help and harm people. Many roots give people food. Other roots can damage houses.

Roots are where a plant stores its food. The plant makes food with its leaves using sunlight. Then the plant stores the food in its roots ready to help the plant grow later. That is why many roots make nourishing food for people.

The roots people eat are called root vegetables. People dig root vegetables out of the ground.

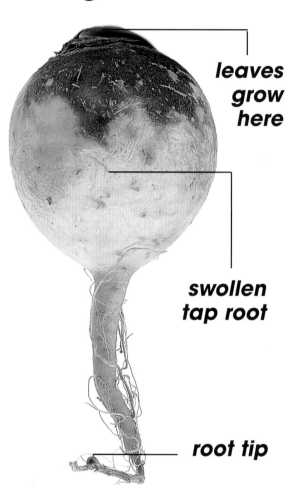

leaves grow here

swollen tap root

root tip

▲ **Turnip**
People have grown turnips to eat for hundreds of years. The part people eat is the plant's large tap root. The leaves grow upward from the root.

It's Amazing!

Not all vegetables that grow underground are roots. Many of them are simply parts of the stem that grow underground for protection. Potatoes are stems, not roots. So too are onions and garlic.

18

The best-known root vegetables in cold and cool countries are carrots, beets, and turnips. In hot countries, many other root vegetables grow, such as yams, sweet potatoes, and cassava.

▲ **Sweet potatoes**
Sweet potatoes are not single tap roots like carrots and beets. They are swollen fibrous roots. People grow sweet potatoes in Africa, South America, and other warm or hot places.

Poisons and medicines

▶ Human ancestors
Millions of years ago, our apelike ancestors probably knew which roots were medicines and which made them ill. Today, animals such as chimpanzees often know this, too.

Some roots are poisonous. The water hemlock looks like a tasty root. But just one bite will kill you. Thousands of years ago, the famous ancient Greek philosopher Socrates was poisoned by hemlock. Mandrake root is poisonous, too. Eating it will not kill you but will make you very sick. It will also give you nightmares. In the past, people thought it had magical properties. They said it squealed when pulled out of the ground.

It's Amazing!

Chinese traditional medicine uses many different roots, such as ginseng, angelica, aconite, and swallowwort. Each root is believed to help cure a particular illness. Wild yam root is supposed to help stomachs. The roots are usually dried and chopped up. Then hot water is poured over them to make tea.

Healing roots

Many roots are thought to make good medicines, including ginseng, echinacea, goldenseal, and black cohosh. People in some parts of the world have used such roots as medicine for hundreds of years. Scientists are now starting to study such plant medicines to see if and how they work. It may be that some of the wonder drugs of the future will be based on chemicals taken from roots.

Powerful roots

Roots may sometimes look weak, but tree roots can be very strong. As they slowly grow, they can crack solid rock. They can break open concrete. They can even knock down brick walls. When people plant trees, they have to make sure the trees are not too close to buildings. If the roots grow too close, they could damage the buildings.

◀ Back to roots

This ancient temple in Cambodia was made of huge blocks of stone hundreds of years ago. The roots of a tree have torn the temple apart.

Glossary

adventitious root a root that grows from a plant's stem.

aerial root a root that grows high in the air on trees and walls.

cell a tiny compartment too small to see. All living things are made of cells.

fibrous roots threadlike roots that spread out in all directions.

primary root a plant's thickest root and the first to grow.

prop roots a root that grows out from the side of a plant to prop (hold) it up.

root hair a thin hairlike side root on a larger root.

root vegetable a vegetable which is actually the root of a plant, like a turnip.

secondary roots the thinner roots that grow off a plant's larger, primary root.

seed pod a hard covering holding a plant's seeds.

stem the long upright stick of a plant that holds the leaves and branches up.

tap root a large primary root that grows deep into the soil.

Find out more

Books

June Loves. *Vegetables (Plants).* Langhorne, Pennsylvania: Chelsea Clubhouse, 2005.
Sally Morgan. *Roots, Stems and Leaves.* New York: Chrysalis, 2004.

Web sites

The Great Plant Escape
www.urbanext.uiuc.edu/gpe
Sprouting Bean Book
www.EnchantedLearning.com/subjects/plants/books/sproutingbean

Index